DE PAOLA, TOMIE.
NOAH AND THE ARK /

C1983.
37565005441513   CENT

P9-ECW-462

UNIVERSITY
PRODUCTS, INC.

Noah and the Ark

Retold and Illustrated
by Tomie dePaola

Winston Press

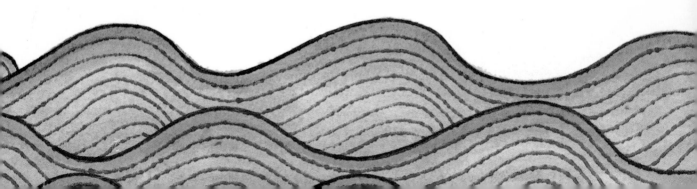

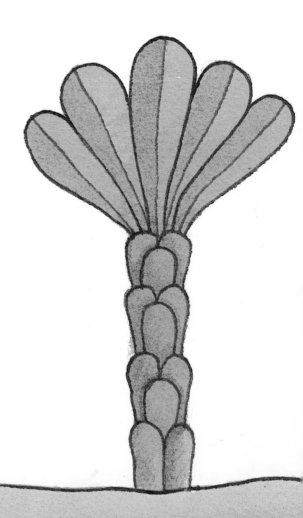

Copyright © 1983 by Tomie dePaola.
All rights reserved. No part of this book may be
reproduced in any form without written permission
from Winston Press.

Paperback edition (with cutouts) ISBN: 0-86683-699-3
Hardback edition ISBN: 0-86683-819-8

Printed in the United States of America.

Series design by Evans-Smith & Skubic Incorporated

5 4 3 2 1

Winston Press, Inc.
430 Oak Grove
Minneapolis, MN 55403

This is the story of Noah.

After the world was made, the people began to forget God.
They lived wicked lives and did bad things.
Only Noah was a good man,
and it was said that he walked with God.

Now, God saw that the whole world was bad
and God was angry.
So God said to Noah,
"I shall destroy the world and all the bad people in it—
all except you, Noah, you and your family.
Build an ark with beams of cypress wood.
Cover it with reeds and coat it inside and out with tar
so no water will get in.

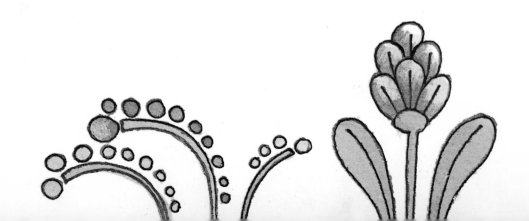

"I shall send a flood that will destroy the whole world
and all the creatures and all the human beings that live in it.
But you and your family,
your wife and your sons and your sons' wives,
shall go into the ark.
You shall also take with you two of every kind of creature—
birds and reptiles and animals—male and female.
And take food with you for you and all the creatures."

So Noah did what God said.

When the ark was built, God spoke again to Noah.
"In seven days," God said, "the rain will begin.
It will rain for forty days and forty nights.
The water will cover the earth.
Take your family and the creatures into the ark and wait."

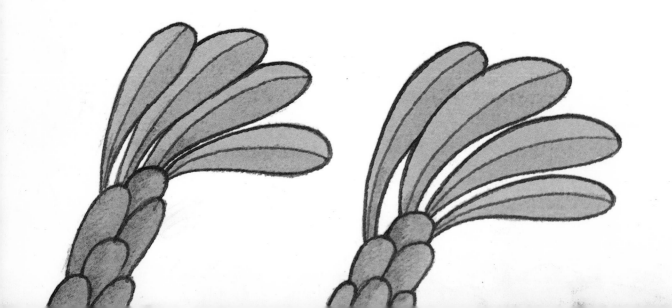

So Noah did what God said.

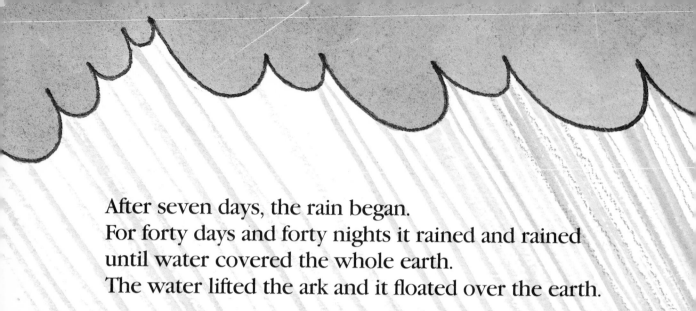

After seven days, the rain began.
For forty days and forty nights it rained and rained
until water covered the whole earth.
The water lifted the ark and it floated over the earth.

The flood waters covered even the highest mountains,
and not one person or one creature on earth was left alive,
just as God said.
But Noah, his family, and the ark floated and tossed
for one hundred and fifty days.

Then God remembered Noah and his family
and all the creatures with him,
and God sent a wind over the earth to dry up the flood.
The water began to go down.

Every day the water went down
until the ark came to rest
on a mountain in Ararat.

Noah opened the trapdoor he had made in the ark
and let loose a raven to see if the earth was dry.
The raven flew back and forth
because it could not find dry ground.

After seven days, Noah let loose a dove,
but the dove could not find a place to rest,
so it came back to the ark.

Seven days later,
he let the dove loose again.
This time it came back
with a branch of an olive tree in its beak.

Noah waited seven more days.
Once more he let the dove loose,
and this time it did not come back.
Noah knew that the earth was dry again.

God said to Noah, "Come out of the ark.
You and your wife, your sons and their wives.
Bring out all the creatures,
the birds, the reptiles, and the animals.
I give them to you, with all growing things.
Let them swarm all over the earth
and be fruitful and multiply."

So Noah did as God said.

Then God made a promise that never again would the world be destroyed by water.

And so, when the skies are cloudy and rain falls,
God puts a rainbow in the sky
to show that the promise will never be broken.